LONDON

Julia A. Royston

BK Royston Publishing
P. O. Box 4321
Jeffersonville, IN 47131
502-802-5385
http://www.bkroystonpublishing.com
bkroystonpublishing@gmail.com

© Copyright – 2024

All Rights Reserved. No part of this book may be reproduced, stored in a retrieval system, or transmitted by any means without the written permission of the author.

Cover Design and Image of London Designed by: Cameron T. Wilson

ISBN-13: 978-1-963136-91-3

Printed in the United States of America

Dedication

I dedicate this book to every creative person on the planet especially the dancers.

You're special.

You're unique.

You're a creative.

Remember that Creatives CREATE!

Acknowledgements

First, I acknowledge my Creator for giving me all of my gifts and especially my gift to write.

My husband who is always supportive, loving and encouraging me to utilize all of my gifts and talents. Thank you honey.

To my mother, Dr. Daisy Foree, who is my number one cheerleader and always tells me, "hang in there, you can do it." To my father, Dr. Jack Foree, who is never far away from me in spirit or my heart. I only have to look in the mirror each day to see him.

To Rev. Claude and Mrs. Lillie Royston who support me in everything I do.

To the rest of my family, I love you and thank you for your prayers, support and love.

To the team of BK Royston Publishing and Royal Media and Publishing that make it easier for me to write and publish the books I love, thank you!

Table of Contents

Dedication	iii
Acknowledgements	v
Jaylynn	ix
Introduction	xi
Meet London	1
Jaylynn and Jackie	13
Learning from the Teacher	23
Win What?!	31
Choosing a Stage	43
For the Love of Dance	61
Thank You!	69
About the Author	71
More Books by this Author	73

Jaylynn

Meet Jaylynn Harris, a real creative and the daughter of two creative parents. Ms. Wright, her teacher has given the class the assignment of making a presentation using any of their creative skills, music, art, dance, singing or writing. Jaylynn is nervous but her two friends, London and Jackie are ready. This book is designed to encourage, inspire and empower creatives everywhere. Creatives create.
Let's go!

Julia A. Royston

Purchase at:
www.roystonchildrenbookstore.com

Jaylynn

The book that started it all is Jaylynn. Jaylynn is London's friend and fellow creative.

Meet Jaylynn Harris, a real creative and the daughter of two creative parents. Ms. Wright, her teacher has given the class the assignment of making a presentation using any of their creative skills, music, art, dance, singing or writing. Jaylynn is nervous but her two friends, London and Jackie are ready. This book is designed to encourage, inspire and empower creatives everywhere. Creatives create. Let's go!

To purchase your copy of Jaylynn, the book and sketchbook, visit www.roystonchildrenbookstore.com

Introduction

My purpose for writing this book is to shine a light and encourage the creatives of this world to keep going and create what's in your head and what only your heart can see and feel.

I have been a creative all of my life. From music to writing books, it's down inside of me. I see it, I hear it and I feel it. Hopefully, the things that I see and feel come through my music and my writings. I guess I'm a little selfish and understand how it feels to be a creative and see other people in the BIG spotlight and only a dim shadow falls on the real creatives behind the scenes. Not anymore!

I see the great potential, intelligence and natural ability that lies in the next generation. I want to make sure that they have the encouragement and continue to have the courage to keep going and growing.

I always want to write, share and publish books that help bring the greatness out of each of you and for the world to see.

Come on creatives, create! Come out of the shadows and into the light! Let the creative light that is within you shine bright!

Takes one to know one.

Let's go!

Julia A. Royston

Meet London

"London, slow down and stop twirling in the living room. You are going to hurt yourself or get dizzy and break something!" her mother said.

"I love twirling, Mama."

"I know you do but not in your grandmother's house with so many delicate and breakable things sitting around."

"Don't worry, Mona. She's just three and not big enough to do much damage," London's grandmother said.

"Who are you, and what have you done with my mother who would yell at us if we sat on the floor with a glass of water instead of at the kitchen table?"

"You were my child. This is my granddaughter."

"Oh, how times have changed."

"Don't be jealous, Mona. I'm older and love to see my granddaughter use her gift and be herself. Listen, if she breaks something, we'll clean it up and then go outside to practice some more."

"Oh, Mama, you need to stop taking up for her. That's what happens when people have grandchildren; they let them get away with a lot of things," Mona replied.

"True, but I'm the grandmother, and I decide because you are still in my house."

"Thank you, Granny!" London said.

"Welcome, but be careful."

"I will."

London kept dancing closer, in the middle of the floor rather than near that very tall cabinet with all of that fine China, intricate glassware and other mementos from her grandmother's travels. When Mona was still carrying London in her stomach, she would put on soft, classical music and London would start kicking on the left side and then the right. Was she dancing? Only London knows that, but her mother could feel the result of just that soft music playing in the background.

Mona wished that London's father could see her dancing. He would have loved it. He would have been on the dance floor with her and shared in all of her adventures, but unfortunately, he passed away when she was two. Mona smiled at the memory but so much in the present of watching her daughter. She quickly wiped away a tear in spite of her smile but happy that London was healthy, happy and loved to dance.

One day while London's mom Mona was at work, her friend came by her desk and said, "Mona, here is a community dance class starting in the summer. The child just has to be five years old to start. Isn't London five?"

"Yes, she just turned five last month, but how much does it cost?"

"Look at the paper; it looks like it's free, but you have to buy some tights or something and maybe a tutu or whatever they are called. You should call and check it out," her friend said.

"I believe I will," Mona answered.

"That baby has twirled and spun in this office, your house and your mama's house so much that her body is screaming dance. You've got to build up and encourage those natural gifts as much as possible."

"I agree. That's what my mama says all of the time, to encourage her gift. Thanks, I'll give them a call," Mona said.

She sat right down and made the call. Sure enough, the class was free but there may be some uniforms or outfits that she would have to buy. Between her and her mother, she would figure it out.

A few weeks later, she surprised London with her favorite personal pan pizza and movie, *The Nutcracker*, even though it was not Christmas time.

"My favorite, Mom. Thank you!" London exclaimed excitedly when she saw the pizza.

"You're welcome, and after dinner, we are going to watch your favorite movie, *The Nutcracker,*" Mom said.

"Great! All of my favorites. What's going on, Mom? It's not my birthday; that was last month," London asked.

"I am glad you noticed, but I'll tell you after we eat and the dishes are done,"

"I can't wait," London squealed as she clapped her hands and did a twirl right there in the kitchen.

With the dishes done, both of them settled on the couch, and with the remote in her hand, Mona said, "Okay, the surprise is I have enrolled you into a dance class at the community center."

"For real?"

"For real."

"Yes. Yes!!" London said as she jumped off the couch and did a dance in the family room.

"Okay, okay," her mom said with a smile, "sit back down, so I can tell you the details."

"Oh, Mom, please tell me. I can hardly wait. When does it start? Where is it? How long is it? Tell me, Tell me!" London shouted.

Mona laughed hysterically, seeing London's excitement. "I'll tell you when you sit down and listen."

"Okay," London said as she finally calmed herself enough to sit back down on the couch.

Mona explained all of the details of the class and where the community center was. Though it was a few weeks away, London bugged her mother every day until it was actually time to go to the first dance class.

When they arrived, Ms. Bell was the dance teacher along with some older teenagers who were there to assist the first class. There had to be about twenty five-year-olds in the class. A lot for any one person to handle alone as they were inexperienced and it was their first time in an actual dance class. The room was large but not overwhelming. There were mirrors all around and horizontal handrails attached to the walls that Mona and London now know are barres. These barres or bars are usually made of wood or metal. Some were taller, for the older or adult dancers. Others were shorter and portable, for the young dancers. The class was on Saturday morning. Mona was off work, and London couldn't sleep the night before, because she was so excited about her first dance class.

"Good morning, everyone. Let's have a seat on the floor first," Ms. Bell said.

All of the little ones sat down on the floor. They were nervous—all of the mothers sitting in the chairs on the opposite wall could tell—but they were paying attention.

"The first thing and most important thing for a dancer is to warm up. All right, so follow me," Ms. Bell said and began showing all of the dancers, including the teenagers, the warm up exercises with the hands, feet, knees and shoulders all working together, even on the floor.

London raised her hand and asked, "When are we going to dance?"

"Oh my, we have an eager one today. Young lady, what is your name?"

"London."

"London, like the famous city in England?"

"Yes, ma'am. That's what my grandmother named me because she visited there once long ago."

"Well, I'm sure she had a wonderful time," Ms. Bell said.

"She did. She said that she—"

"Oh, I'm sorry we don't have time for a story today, but maybe some other time. We came here to learn all about the important parts and steps in dance and that's what we're going to do. All right?"

"All right," London replied. A little disappointed, her mother could tell, because she was about to go straight into the London bridges or the Big Ben story that her grandmother had often told her since she was two years old.

About twenty minutes later, the teacher said, "Everyone, let's stand."

London raised her hand again. "Now, do we get to dance?"

"Yes, London, we will get to dance."

"Yes!" London shouted.

Everyone in the room giggled, but Ms. Bell knew that she would have to watch out for London because she was outspoken and talented but could easily take over her class if she let her.

As Mona waited for London to get home from school with a cup of coffee in her hand, she thought back on those early days of London's life and how much she loved to twirl and dance. As a child, Mona always loved music, and now that same love of music plus dance had not only transferred, but clearly taken over her daughter, London.

Living in the city where classical music, the theater, and dance studios were everywhere, as well as other art forms as close as walking a short distance out of the front door of their brownstone house, to easily enjoy and encourage the love of music and dance because of the ease of access.

Now, eight years later, and London's love of music and just twirling free-style had grown to her performing on stage. Her mother's hope was that she learned all aspects of the dance world for the present and her future.

Jaylynn and Jackie

Mona's phone rang, and by the ring tone, she knew it was London. "Hey, London, what's up?"

"Hey, Mom, can Jaylynn and Jackie come over after school? We're working on a project together and I thought they could come to our house."

"Do their parents know?"

"Yes."

"I didn't get a call from either of their mothers," Mona said.

"I'm sorry, but they said yes, I promise."

"Ask Jaylynn and Jackie to tell their mothers to text me their approval and then they can come over. Are they going to pick them up, or will I have to take them home?"

"They'll pick them up later," London said.

"Okay, but I need to see a text before they walk through the door, young lady."

"Yes, ma'am."

"You guys must have cooked this up at school."

"It just seemed easier since it's Friday. I have dance tomorrow. We would be together in the same room, instead of online trying to see each other while we work on this project, like we had to do during COVID," London explained.

"I agree and understand, but we still need their mothers' permission. Be careful."

"Yes, ma'am," London said as she hung up the phone and turned to her best friends. "My mom says that you both have to have your mothers text my mom that's it's okay."

"Just give us the number," Jaylynn said. "You know my mom's home."

"My mom is too," Jackie said.

London gave them the number, and Mona quickly got two text messages which she replied to, feeling better about London's best friends coming to the house.

Once they arrived at the house, it was all chatter. Mona had light snacks on the table, bottles of water and hugs all around.

"Okay, girls, I'm going to leave you guys to your work. Clean up the kitchen and be sure and say goodbye before you leave."

"Yes, ma'am," they said in unison.

After they had their snacks and cleaned up the kitchen, the upstairs family room was where they headed. It was situated up some narrow stairs, like an attic, but it had been arranged and multi-purposed to be a third bedroom for London to sleep in when guests visited and a storage and work room for London to study, create and dance.

"I love this room, London," Jaylynn said.

"Me too," Jackie agreed.

"Me three, because it is private, roomy and mine, kind of," London told them.

"That's the best part."

They all giggled.

"Okay, so this is a new project. Last year's project was a hit and got a good grade and did get us noticed in the community, but this is for the community competition project," London began.

"The theme is *The City's Got Talent*," one of the other girls added.

"I love that, but it leaves it wide open too.

"Which is also a little scary."

"But exciting, too, because we can do our own thing and not have to stick with rigid school guidelines," London pointed out.

"Jackie, what did you have in mind?"

"I've been working on a song. It's got an African beat to it, called *Home*. Really simple melody and simple words, so Jaylynn can easily put her own writing to it or draw something, if you like," Jackie said as she looked over at Jaylynn.

"Well, you know I've got to hear it so I can feel it and, hopefully, create the dances to it," London said.

"You are so good at that, London."

"Yeah, I love creating my own dances, but my ballet teacher sure doesn't like it."

"How does that work out?"

"I am restricted. I dance what and how they tell me to dance."

"That's okay, I guess, but your creations are good, too, and should somehow be spotlighted," Jackie said.

"Maybe one day."

"No, it's going to be in a few weeks, at this *City's Got Talent* show," Jaylynn said.

"Right."

"Exactly."

They worked for two hours straight, hashing out ideas, listening to Jackie's incredible song, London moving about the room and Jaylynn drawing what she saw as well as putting some captions down under the pictures. It was a creatives dream, no arguments, just ideas flowing.

London and her mom stood at the door waving good bye to her friends and their moms. They would see each at school on Monday, but with permission, of course, they agreed to do this again every Friday, to practice and get everything perfected until the competition in a few weeks.

"So, how did it go, London?" Mona asked.

"Great, Mom."

"I didn't hear any arguments or anything coming from upstairs, just your feet twirling across the floor."

"Nope, we get along so well, and I love working with them. We make a good team," London said.

"That's great."

"But, Mom, I don't always work well with my ballet teacher, Ms. Britt. She is so hard on me and never likes my suggestions."

"Remember, Ms. Britt is the teacher and you are the student. You may think that you have an idea that is great or better, but she is still the teacher and in charge, so listen to her."

"I guess."

"No, don't guess, but understand that you are still learning. She has been on stages literally around the world. She is the teacher and you should learn from her, no matter what it looks like or feels like. Do you know how many bosses I didn't agree with but went along with their suggestions because they were in charge? Now, I will soon be in charge of my own consulting business and the things that they taught me. I am going to use them, even though, back then, I didn't agree."

"I get it, but it is hard to not want to do my own thing and dance the way that I feel it instead of the choreography that is set."

"Don't ever stop wanting to dance your own way, but right now, you need the fundamentals, to hone your craft and take your raw talent and better it with a great instructor. You have forgotten that quickly that you *are* getting the chance to do it your way with this project and competition with Jaylynn and Jackie, right?"

"Right."

"Remember, Ms. Bell used to do the same thing and you learned from her. Now, you're older and you're going to learn from Ms. Britt, the way she wants you to do it for her stage. Then, take the knowledge that your teacher gives you and express it however you want on your own stage with Jaylynn and Jackie. Understand?"

"Yes, ma'am, and great idea."

"How about we watch a silly movie or cartoon before we go to bed?"

"Sounds like another great idea. You're the best, Mom."

"I try, love, I try." Mona was worried about her daughter being overwhelmed by these teachers, but life didn't always go like you want or how you want. London had to learn that too.

Learning from the Teacher

The next day, London and her mom arrived a little early for dance class.

"Good morning, Ms. Britt."

"Good morning, London. You are here early."

"Yes, I wanted to get here early to warm up before everyone else came."

"Sounds good, sounds good. We'll get started with real warm ups in about fifteen minutes."

"Yes, ma'am."

"Ms. Britt, do you have a minute?" Mona asked.

"Sure, Ms. Fairfield, come into my office."

"Have a seat. How can I help you?"

"Well, I am wondering, starting to plan moving forward, how you believe that London is doing with her dancing?"

"Well, I believe that London is a wonderful dancer, naturally, but I don't know how serious she really is in the fundamentals or advancing her skills technically."

"What exactly do you mean? We come to the dance classes regularly, pay the fees and purchase the uniforms. Is there another level of serious that she needs to get to?"

"To be frank and honest, London doesn't have the body type for a prima ballerina. She would need to be taller and much slimmer."

"She barely eats now. She works out. She practices in her own upstairs studio every day. How much more does she need to do?"

"She needs to lose at least twenty pounds for a young man to be able to lift her weight."

"She weighs 110 now. So, you need her to be under 100 pounds?"

"Absolutely," the teacher said.

"Is that healthy?"

"Let me explain it this way. Just like a boxer or other athlete, there are things that you have to do to your body to maintain it."

"My daughter is not a boxer, football player or sumo wrestler. She is a dancer and has danced on her own since she was able to walk. I thought you would suggest a particular workout regimen or diet that she should eat to stay healthy but not starve the girl to death."

"Not starving, but maintaining a proper weight for dance. London has the skill for a lead but not the body type, frame or size for a lead role," Ms. Britt explained.

"So, all of this is for nothing?"

"No, she'll always cast in a ballet production, just probably never the lead. That's something you and she will have to sit down and decide, your next steps."

"Always in the background, but never in the foreground as a main lead."

"It can happen, but probably not in this dance studio or company."

"Thank you for your honesty."

"You're welcome."

Mona Fairfield walked out of Ms. Britt's office crushed for her daughter. She knew that London had talent and would one day be on stages around the world, but with this piece of information, she knew that she would have to be looking for somewhere else for London to dance or be taught that would build up her skills without trying to starve her, which would jeopardize her health, self-esteem and gift.

When Mona sat down, she was still staring off into space, but also at her daughter who was warming up with the other students.

Suddenly, London went into a move, up on her toes, her arms stretched out wide and her palms pointed up.

"London! What are you doing?" Ms. Britt yelled from across the room, just a few feet from her office door.

"Nothing, just something I thought I would try."

"Try on your own time. That move didn't look like anything that I taught in this class. These classes are for the choreography that I produce, approve and want to see perfected. Now, let's begin formal warm-ups and take the dance from the top."

Everything in Mona wanted to jump out of the chair, grab London by the hand and leave, but she took her cues from London. London turned her back to the others, gathered her composure and turned around with her head up, ready to do her part.

What's a mother to do?

I can't protect her from everything. If you quit every time something gets hard, you would be quitting everything and not accomplishing much of anything. Life is hard, and this is one of those hard times that

London must go through, or not?' Mona's mind was racing and she was fighting worry.

On the way home, London asked, "Mom, you alright?"

"Yes, I'm good," she replied, which Mona and London both knew was a lie, but she gave London a fake smile as best she could.

"Ms. Britt was hard on us today."

"Yes, she was very hard on you all today, but teachers can be hard because they want to get the best performance as possible. I have had bosses and supervisors who have been hard on the entire team or department. They said that it wasn't personal, but it was still hurtful, the things said and done. We have to look at it from her perspective. She is looking at the overall performance, the business of running a studio and the future of all of it. Also, we live in a world that doesn't really support the creative arts as they should. So, it is hard on everyone, from the owners, teachers, supports to the artists themselves. London, you are an excellent student and can get a scholarship to do anything in this world that you desire. My question to you is how much do you love dancing, and would you like to do it full time?" Mona asked.

"I love it and would love to do it full-time. I realize that I can't do it for life, past thirty-years-old, but I want to dance as long as I can. Mommy, I live to dance. I see myself dancing while I sleep. I hear music and my body wants to move," London said.

"That's all I needed to know," Mona replied.

Win What?!

Over the next several weeks, the practices continued with London and her friends for the community competition as well as the strict practices and choreography preparing for the ballet recital with Ms. Britt.

London did her very best in all of it. Her body was tired, but this was what she loved and wouldn't trade the hard work for anything.

It was Saturday and the last rehearsal for the recital. London and her mom headed to the studio and noticed there were some extra guests at the studio. They were early, as usual, so they wondered why all of the people. The warm ups hadn't begun because the dancers were still arriving.

"What's going on? Was there an email that I missed?" Mona asked one of the other mothers.

"I don't really know, but we have a lot of outsiders. If you missed the email, I did, too, because I didn't get a notification of anything extra. I guess Ms. Britt will let us all know," the other mom replied.

"I guess so." Mona was kind of worried but excited along with the other moms and the dancers.

Suddenly, Ms. Britt clapped her hands, which was unusual, but everything was this Saturday morning.

"Good morning, everyone. For our guests, I'm Ms. Judith Britt, the director of the studio, and welcome! To the dancers, go ahead, get ready and warm up just like we always do. We have about thirty minutes before I will explain further, but don't get distracted or nervous about our guests. Imagine that you are on the stage at the night of the recital. There will be even more people there than are here this morning. Continue…"

"Molly, you know who all of these people are?" London asked one of the other students.

"No, London, but they are making me nervous. You know how I am right before we go on stage."

"I understand, but I guess we'll soon find out."

"Yes, I guess so. I just don't want to mess up," Molly said.

"Me, either," London agreed.

The arrivals and warmups continued for the next thirty minutes while everyone in the room wondered what was going on.

Thirty minutes later, right on the dot, Ms. Britt got the room's attention again.

"Can I have your attention please? I want to introduce the students, their parents and the media to our special guest. She is in town from London and on staff with their phenomenal ballet company there. She is in town as a judge for the City-Wide Community Creative Arts Competition. She is a personal friend of mine and esteemed colleague. It is my pleasure to introduce you all to Ms. Kateland Royalton." Ms. Britt clapped her hands, which began the applause for everyone else in the room, with the biggest smile on her face. It was so unlike her. London rarely saw her smile, so the guest must be someone extra special.

The video cameras began rolling and the flash on the photographers' cameras was almost blinding.

Molly whispered, "I guess I'll have to Google her."

"Me too," London replied. She knew that she had been so busy preparing for the recital, doing her school work and the community project with Jaylynn and Jackie that there was very little time for anything else, especially social media.

"Greetings to you all. I am pleased as punch to be here with you, but especially with my friend, Ms. Britt, and home, in the dance studio. Don't mind me. Carry on and do what you do best. I am thrilled to be here and look forward to seeing you prepare for your dance recital. It brings back more memories than you can imagine. Thank you so much for allowing me to be here. Have a great show!" Ms. Royalton said.

"Thank you again for being here. All right, boys and girls, get in position and let's see you in action," Ms. Britt said.

Mona Fairfield held her breath while keeping a close eye on her daughter but watching all of the dance students. It was a pleasure to know that someone famous and important was actually in the same studio with her daughter. It was exposure, a performance, and maybe an opportunity.

"Let's begin," Ms. Britt said through clenched teeth and with a nod in the music director's direction.

It was apparent to all who were watching that Ms. Britt was nervous, but also anxious to show off the dancers to her guest, as well as to the camera and videography crew that was on hand for the rehearsal. It added to everyone's anxiety, but Ms. Britt was especially on edge.

After a few minutes of watching from the front of the room, Ms. Royalton began moving about the room. She was toward the back where London was dancing. She suddenly stopped and was clearly observing all of the dancers, but especially London. She walked directly to London in mid-movement and asked, "Excuse me, young lady, what is your name?" Ms. Royalton asked.

Ms. Britt was definitely close by. "Her name is London, but please come back and observe the older girls up front."

London was not able to utter her own name before Ms. Britt had interrupted.

"No, I'm fine, Britt, right here. I'll come back up front in a moment," Ms. Royalton said.

"Very well," Ms. Britt said very tightly.

"Now, let me ask you again. What is your name, dear?" Ms. Royalton asked again.

"London Fairfield."

"Nice to meet you, London Fairfield. How long have you been dancing?"

"Here with Ms. Britt, or at home as well?"

"Both."

"I've been at the Britt Studio for two years. My mother says that I've been dancing since before I could walk and I'm thirteen-years-old," London replied.

"Well-spoken, and you dance very well. Do you enjoy dancing?" Ms. Royalton replied with a chuckle.

"Yes, ma'am, very much," London said.

"I can tell. Keep dancing, and don't ever stop," Ms. Royalton replied.

"Thank you," London said with a smile.

"Coming, Britt. I'm coming," Ms. Royalton said as she walked away.

London immediately found her place in the dance and rejoined the others. Mona just smiled at her daughter because she didn't want to throw her off from the dance routine and cause any more attention to her than the guest had already.

Once the dance routine was done, the dancers were praised and a few got some encouragement, but not like London. The dancers were gracious, went to change clothes and prepared to leave.

Mona stayed in her place until London changed and came out to the main floor. She overheard Ms. Royalton talking to Ms. Britt.

"What do you have against the young London dancer, she good?"

"I just don't think that she has what it takes physically to be a prima dancer."

"You don't think, or you know she doesn't have what it takes?"

"At this point, I think," Britt replied.

"That's sounds better, and I think your traditional eyes of what ballet dancers should look like is showing. I understand it, but I don't always agree with it. Ballet dancers have normally had a specific look as well as a gift, but I believe that today's ballet dancers don't fit a mold, cookie cutter or replica all of the time. Everyone should have the fundamentals of the dance moves, positions, frame and even background, history of the art form, but making everyone look alike, dance alike and be alike, I believe is too restrictive, my friend."

Ms. Britt made no response back to her friend. It was evident that her style was not accepted or promoted in the overall dance world. In a few clicks, Mona found out just how famous and influential that Ms. Royalton was but didn't want to overstep and introduce herself. In the back of her mind, she knew that London's hard work, dedication and love of dance would get her noticed and not be dependent on her saying or doing anything unless it was absolutely necessary.

On the way home, Mona asked her daughter about the conversation. "So, what did Ms. Royalton said to you?"

"She asked my name and Ms. Britt cut her off, but she asked me my name again. I told her, and then she asked me if I enjoyed dance. I said yes, and she said that she could tell. Finally, Mama, she said, 'Keep dancing; don't stop,'" London said.

"That's wonderful and very encouraging," Mona said.

"Yes, Mama, it was encouraging, but I was still nervous."

"That's understandable, but that is a part of being in the arts, on stage and performing. Being nervous. I'm nervous every day, about so many things, but I keep going."

"Just like Ms. Royalton said that I have to keep dancing."

"Absolutely. Let me tell you this; if you quit every time you get nervous, scared or have a problem, you'll always be quitting. I didn't birth or raise a quitter. Quitting something and being a quitter are two different things. Sometimes you quit things because they no longer serve, the time has ended, the season is over, the class ended or you no longer do it. Being a quitter, means that you never get to the end, fulfill the assignment, solve the problem, put in the work and get through the hard part enough to complete anything. That, my friends, is *not* my daughter," Mona said.

"Thanks, Mom."

"You're welcome. What do you want for dinner?" Mona asked, changing the subject.

"I want a meal. Meat, vegetables, potatoes and a roll, with a piece of pie for dessert."

"Wow, somebody's hungry," Mona said.

"Me, that's who," London replied as she laughed.

"Well, fortunately for you, young lady, your grandmother has that very meal all prepared for us and we are headed there now."

"Great!"

They arrived at London's grandmother's house for food, fun and a lot of conversation. The night ended with London's favorite chocolate pie, her grandmother's specialty.

"Good night, you two. Remember what I said about Fairfields never quitting; they just keep going until the job is done."

"Yes, ma'am. Good night," London said.

"Good night, Mom, and thanks for dinner."

Choosing a Stage

For the next two weeks, there were two final rehearsals and a dress rehearsal for the Britt Company recital, which would be held prior to the community event with London, Jaylynn and Jackie.

The community event was a competition, so they kept all of the details quiet and only the girls and their parents knew the details.

At their last rehearsal, London asked, "Do you think we need to actually be on a stage to be more comfortable, or are you guys good with what we have?"

"I'm good with my part but, Jackie, how do you feel?" Jaylynn asked.

"I would love to have a sound system, to know how the music is going to sound in the auditorium, but that is money, coordination and timing. I think we need to just go with what we have, especially since you you're your recital literally the night before our performance," Jackie added, looking at London.

"I agree, but the stage is going to be so much larger than this attic space. I will have to wing it when we get up there."

"We do have a dress rehearsal and microphone check the day before, so that can work."

"The only problem is I have a dress rehearsal on Thursday night, the performance on Friday, and then our performance on Saturday. When would we rehearse?"

"Tuesday or Wednesday maybe?" Jackie asked.

"I'm good on Tuesday or Wednesday, but what about you, London?"

"I'll have to ask my mom," London replied.

They all three headed down to the kitchen where Mona was preparing dinner.

"Okay, Ms. Fairfield, we have a problem," Jackie said.

"Yes, Mom, we have a problem," London chimed in.

"What is it?" Mona asked.

"We need to practice the dance on a full stage before the community event," London explained.

"You probably do need to hear the music and everything. Let me see if I can arrange something at school. I am pretty cool with you guys' principal and music teacher. Let me ask."

"We only have a week," London reminded her.

"I understand, but there are no productions going on right now at school, so we should be good. Let me ask on Monday. What day?"

"Can it be after school on Tuesday or Wednesday?"

"I'll ask. They can only say yes or no," Mona replied.

"Thank you."

"Now, girls, get your stuff. Your moms should be here any moment."

"Yes, ma'am," they replied in unison.

Mona arranged it with the principal, the plant operator and the music teacher at their school to allow them one hour to practice after school on the stage on Wednesday. All of the students would be gone and the teachers would be leaving the building as well.

Mid-way through the practice, which was going well, the doors opened and ten adults came through the door. The adults were fellow dance, music and theatre performers and directors, meeting with Ms. Royalton and touring the various stages in the city. In the group, were Ms. Britt and Ms. Royalton, who was still in town conducting interviews and networking for her International Summer Dance camp that would be held within the next three months.

"Oh my, that looks like that fabulous dancer, London, on the stage. I wonder what she is working on."

"London, London Fairfield."

"Looks like the same London. Britt, I have to go say hello. Excuse me, everyone. I must go say hello to the young women on the stage," Ms. Royalton said.

Ms. Britt was rushing behind Ms. Royalton as she walked toward the stage. "Good evening, ladies. London, who are these other young talented ladies?"

"Hello," they all said.

"Hi, Ms. Royalton and Ms. Britt, these are my friends, Jaylynn and Jackie. We are practicing for the community event on Saturday evening at City Theatre," London explained.

"Wonderful," Ms. Royalton said.

"That is not wonderful. London, isn't that too much for you, to participate in the recital on Friday and then the community thing on Saturday?"

"No, ma'am, I will be fine."

"I don't like it. I don't think that you should do both. In my opinion you really need to choose. By the way, who is the choreographer for this performance?"

"I am," London replied.

"You are? What do you know about choreography?" Ms. Britt said.

"I just dance what I hear and feel. I put the steps together. Jaylynn writes the words and does spoken word. Jackie makes the music and sings. I dance. We've been doing this all of the years of middle school. This is our first community competition."

"Well said, London. Britt, isn't that what you do, dance what you feel?" Ms. Royalton said.

"Kate, you know that I am classically trained. I am a dance major and not an amateur, dancing by what I hear and feel."

"That's too bad, because that is what a true choreographer should be doing. Dancing to the music to create mood, creating a scene or visual, as it were, to draw people in, rather than relying totally on just academic training and book skill."

"I think not. I am the owner of Britt Dance Studio and I have the say on who dances and who does not dance."

Just then, Mona Fairfield walked in. "Everything all right here?"

"No, it's not. I didn't know that your daughter has been doing her own performances on the side, outside of the Britt Studio."

"I'm sorry, Ms. Britt, but I was unaware that we had to tell you when, where and how London dances outside of your dance studio. We follow your instructions and steps while at the studio and for your performances, but outside of that, it is her business and my business. I don't believe that these young women have done anything wrong."

"I disagree. Choose," Ms. Britt said.

"Choose? What does that mean exactly?" Mona asked.

"Choose between the two performances. It is either the Britt Dance Studio recital on Friday, or this community event thing on Saturday. You can't have both. I will not permit it."

"Britt, you are wrong, and you know it," Ms. Royalton said.

"I don't care what you say, Kate. This is my studio, and I decide. This stops here," Ms. Britt said.

London broke down in tears on stage and was comforted by Jaylynn and Jackie.

"This is terrible, Ms. Britt. After all of the sacrifice, rehearsals, time, clothing bought for the recital, and now she can't be in it because of the community event which is open to anyone who lives in the community? She created her dances, coordinated with her friends, practiced for weeks on her own time, effort and creative leadership, and now, because of your selfish reasoning, you are making her choose. I am her mother. I will consult with her about her decision and we will let you know what we decide. We still have twenty minutes on the stage and we have the principal's permission to be here. Good evening," Ms. Fairfield said as she walked away.

"London, remember what I said," Ms. Royalton yelled out as she walked backward toward the other adult group.

Upon the return to the group, she said, "I'm sorry for the interruption. Can we move forward to the next theatre? I believe that I have seen all that I want to see for now," Ms. Royalton said.

"Kate, what I meant was..." Ms. Britt said as she rushed toward her.

"Not another word, Britt. Not another word," Ms. Royalton said as she waved her hand in front of Ms. Britt to stop her.

The adult arts leadership group immediately left the auditorium.

"We totally understand, London," Jaylynn said.

"I get it. It has cost so much time and money being with the ballet company and all. We feel for you, but we'll understand the decision to not be in the Community Competition because you can't do both," Jackie added.

"It's left up to you, dear," Mona said.

"I don't want to quit either event. I don't know why I can't do them both."

"That is Ms. Britt's decision and although we don't agree with it, she has the final say. She is asking for you to choose one or the other and not both. I'm your mother, and no matter what, I'm with you, whatever you choose."

"Mom, so much money you and Grandma have spent," London pointed out.

"Don't worry about that. The most important thing is that you do what you love and that your heart is in it and don't worry about anything else but that," Mona said.

"You want to wait and let us know later?" Jaylynn asked.

"No, I can't wait. It is Wednesday and dress rehearsal is tomorrow. I choose you guys and the community center event," London said.

"You sure?" Jackie asked.

"You sure?" Mona, her mom asked too.

"I'm disappointed, but I'm sure," London replied.

"So much has happened; do you guys need to go over the performance one more time, or are you good?"

"I'm good," London replied.

"We're good as well," Jackie said and turned to Jaylynn for her agreement.

"Pack up everything and I'll meet you guys in the car. I'm going to let the plant operator know that we're done," Ms. Fairfield said as she walked toward the door, heartbroken for her daughter and her friends. Kids trust adults to make the right decision and not one based on their own selfish reasoning. Mona Fairfield wondered whether this was Ms. Britt's way of quietly dismissing London from the company. It clearly wasn't about her dance skills and ability; it was about loyalty and commitment to her company, rather than to the love of dance.

"Yes, ma'am," they all said at the same time.

The ride home was quiet and there were only soft goodbyes when Jaylynn and Jackie were let out at their respective homes. It was the harsh reality of those adult, "beyond your control" situations.

Meanwhile, across town, Ms. Royalton confronted Ms. Britt on her decision, "You know you are wrong and have scarred a good dancer for life."

"Not for life, just for this recital."

"Why do you think the young woman London would even want to come back to dance at your company?"

"Because we are the best dance studio in the city."

"Maybe the best, but not the only dance studio. What about the other ones that I saw? They were not bad at all. The instructors seemed to be nice, friendly and capable. By the way, what criteria was used when determining the best?"

"I don't really know. Just the newspaper, where my friend is the editor, claimed us to be the best," Britt replied smugly.

"So, it is by default that you are the best and truly haven't earned it, or the people didn't cast a vote?"

"I guess, but we're the best; that's printed in black and white."

"You still haven't told me what you have against this young dancer and why she can't dance in both performances."

"It's a matter of commitment and loyalty to the studio."

"To the studio? What about her commitment to dancing, herself and her gift? Did you not think of that? She has to think of her long-term career in dance. Is she a good student?"

"You know I only accept those who have good grades and dancing ability."

"So, she has options, correct?"

"Correct."

"So, you are controlling and deciding a young girl's opportunity at thirteen-years-old, based on a commitment and loyalty to you when you're not committed and loyal to her."

"How do you mean?"

"It's all about you. Not her talent, not what she wants, and not how far she wants to go in this art form, but how it impacts your studio and reputation. I understand that you are in the dance business, but what cost and price are you really charging? Besides all of the fees, what price are you making her pay, her future? That's too high, don't you think? We're friends, but I have a reputation too. How can I refer people to your studio here in the United States when I know how you treated this one young lady? If we're talking about business, if I don't like the way you treat dancers here, what makes you think that I would want to associate my studio in the United Kingdom with your studio here after I have seen, heard and know your practices. You don't have one valid reason for making that young girl choose, do you?"

"Yes, I do. I said that it was commitment and loyalty."

"No, that's not it. You're selfish, intimidated and jealous."

"No, I'm not," Britt argued.

"Yes, you are. You had your chance. You were a good dancer in your day, but that time has passed. You are now the teacher but one who is now jealous of a student who has the possibility for a great, promising career on the stage, and you got jealous of that. You probably talked to her mom about her weight, like Ms. Angelina did all of our moms back in the day so that we literally starved ourselves to be the lead in an upcoming recital. Healthwise, that is dangerous and not good for young bodies. What you don't understand is that if she loves dance the way I think she loves dance, she will have a wonderful career without you, and I look forward to judging her performance on Saturday night."

"You're judging the competition on Saturday?"

"Absolutely. They just asked me if I would consider being the fourth judge, and I said yes. Surprise, Britt!"

When London and her mom got home, they called her grandmother to fill her in, and this was what she said, "London, my dear, disappointment is painful and jealousy is cruel, but you will dance Saturday night like the world is watching. No more thought of that dance studio, but you and your friends are going to do great on Saturday. You hear me?"

"Yes, ma'am."

"Get some sleep. On Saturday night, I look forward to watching the splendor of the dancing beauty which is my granddaughter who used to twirl all over my house when she was little."

"Yes, ma'am, but it still hurts," London said.

"I know it does, but you only overcome pain and disappointment by being the best. Love you and good night. Get some rest."

Everyone was so exhausted from the day that sleep came easily. Tomorrow was another day and an opportunity to prepare to do what each of them loved.

For the Love of Dance

The next day, London and her mom sat down at the computer and wrote out the email to Ms. Britt stating that they would not be participating in the recital on Friday or continuing with her dance lessons at that studio.

Ten minutes after the email was sent, Ms. Britt called.

"Hello," Mona answered her cell phone and put her on speaker phone so that London could hear.

"Hello, Ms. Fairfield, this is Ms. Britt."

"Hello. You received our email?"

"Yes, I did, and I wanted to say that London doesn't have to quit the dance company altogether, just choose to not dance at both events, that's all."

"How would that benefit London, to just dance with your company and not dance at both events?" Mona asked.

"I guess I don't get what you mean."

"I mean that if she only dances with your company and does not dance in any other competition, event or opportunity, what would be the advantage?"

"I guess that she would benefit by being classically and formally trained by an expert, experienced in the ballet arts so that she can be the best ballet dancer that she can be," Britt replied.

"But when we met, Ms. Britt, you weren't really convinced that London was a good dancer unless she weighed under 100 pounds. Is that correct?"

"I never said that London wasn't a good dancer, I just feel that most good dancers are smaller in body size and weight."

"So, it's not her ability, but the size of her body?"

"I guess."

"That's either a yes or no, Ms. Britt."

"Yes, if you trace back in history, ballerinas have had a certain body type, shape and size, so we want to keep with that tradition."

"It's tradition and not a requirement to be a good dancer, correct?"

"Correct."

"Well, that is not good enough for my daughter. Ms. Britt, you may be an expert, experienced and very knowledgeable, but your tradition could be harmful to my daughter. My daughter is a dancer and has danced since before she could walk. We need to find someone who understands, nurtures and appreciates London for the dancer she is right now and not the dancer that was in the past. Good day, Ms. Britt. Best wishes on a great recital tomorrow. We have work to do," Ms. Fairfield said as she hung up the phone.

Two days later, the big community arts competition arrived. The girls had worked so hard to perfect everything and it was now time to leave everything on the stage and give it their all.

When they arrived, Ms. Fairfield went back stage with them while the other parents found and held her seat. The girls peered from backstage to see the audience. The judges were positioned down front and London noticed that Ms. Royalton was seated with the other judges.

"Ms. Royalton is a judge?" London asked her mom.

"Who is that?" Jaylynn asked.

"Ms. Royalton from where?" Jackie also asked.

"Ms. Royalton is the lady who was at the school the other day," London told them.

"From England?"

"Yes, from England."

"They just announced her as a special surprise guest judge from some big-time studio in England."

"I guess so. What a surprise," Ms. Fairfield said.

"Well, it is time to let her see what JLJ Performance and I are all about," London said.

"That's what I'm talking about," Jackie said.

The introductions were made by a local news anchor and the people cheered after each act, no matter how they performed.

There were exactly ten acts altogether, and JLJ Performance was the ninth act. When the MC announced them from backstage, they clasped hands together, nodded to each other and said, "Let's go." They walked out onto the stage with the lights so bright that they could not actually see the audience and just barely the stage. They positioned themselves, and the music started. Just like they rehearsed it, they started their performance right on cue. Jaylynn started speaking as the narrator, Jackie was humming to the music and London twirled faster than she had as a child and commanded the stage.

Jaylynn's words resonated with everyone in the audience. Jackie sang her heart out to the music that came from Heaven. London danced like the world was truly watching, to the music that she could feel from her head down to her toes.

When they finished, they received a standing ovation. The crowd roared, whistled loudly and stomped their feet to the wood floor, making a sound like the rolling seas.

The three girls hugged each other, wiped tears and bowed, with a smile to the crowd. They did it!

The tenth act didn't go on. One of their performers was sick and they couldn't perform without them, so they forfeited their opportunity.

The MC, or host of the show, asked the judges to come up on stage again and stand to one side while they announced the third, second and first place winners.

He announced the third and second place winners, which were actually very good, but then said, "Finally, the first-place winner is JLJ Performance, to receive the grand prize of $3,000." The girls screamed from backstage and held each other's hands as they walked out onto the stage.

"Congratulations, ladies, please shake the judges' hands and have your parents follow Meredith over there, so she can secure the check, equally divided in each of your names."

"Thank you," they shouted together.

When London shook Ms. Royalton's hand, the woman said, "Please give this to your mother. I want you to come to London for a two-week camp this summer. All expenses paid and housing included. I'll make sure of it. You deserve it."

"Thank you," London said, in awe.

London, Jaylynn and Jackie ran to their parents, and London handed the card to her mom and told her what Ms. Royalton had said. "What do you think, Mom?"

"London, in London. Sounds great to me," Mona said with a smile.

Thank You!

Thank you so much for reading London. This book is dedicated to those in the creative arts. The athletes get so much attention and accolades that I've dedicated the series, Jaylynn, now London, and coming up soon is Jackie.

So if you are a creative person, meaning you write, dance, sing, play an instrument, draw pictures or create videos, audios or any other creative outlet, these books are for you. The world needs all that you have to offer. Keep being great. Keep being a creative. You have a gift and it resides in you. Let's go!

For updates and to stay connected with Julia Royston, visit www.juliaakroyston.com.

About the Author

Julia Royston spends her days doing what she loves, writing, publishing, speaking about her why and motto, "Helping You Get Your Message to the Masses, Turn Your Words into Wealth and Be a Book Business Boss." Julia is the author of 130+ books, published 400+, recorded 3 music CDs and coached more than 350+ to be published authors. She is the owner of five companies, a non-profit organization and the editor of the Book Business Boss Magazine.

To stay connected with Julia, visit www.juliaakroyston.com.

Social Media

Facebook, Instagram, LinkedIN, TikTok and Threads - @juliaaroyston

X - @juliaakroyston

More Books by This Authors

www.ingramcontent.com/pod-product-compliance
Lightning Source LLC
Chambersburg PA
CBHW071203090426
42736CB00012B/2433